Sutures

K B

Presentation by *BookLeaf Publishing*

Web: www.bookleafpub.com

E-mail: info@bookleafpub.com

ISBN: 9789395755146

First edition 2022

A map-maker's nightmare

The unique topography of her face is impossible
to map
Those who dare traverse this land are lost
forever
Each mountain, valley and river is carved by a
tragic truth
Stories told by a voice unknown in a language
encrypted
There are corners that do not know light
Whispers tease of a cursed treasure hidden in
these caves
Shadows dance to songs of danger and treachery
Of a poisoned oasis and bloodcurdling screams
And a midnight sun that burns sweet flesh
There is but one meadow, peaceful and safe and
secret
Only her tears know the way.

CRISIS

Venepuncture. Cannulation.
Airway. Breathing. Circulation.
Vital signs. Acute resuscitation plan.
Paracetamol. Amoxicillin. Riskman.

PANDEMIC

Well's criteria. Roster. Scrum.
Glucose. Once daily. Perforated Ear drum.
Personal Protective Equipment. Scrubbing.
Visual field. Full blood count. Clubbing.

BURNOUT

Sinus rhythm. Plaster of Paris. Slit lamp.
Urine. Radiation. Sterile. Clamp.
Sutures. Lateral. Cervical spine.
Culture. Proprioception. Misalign.

HELP

I, Pencil

If I was a pencil, bear with me here
I'd be the ordinary kind of HB and lead,
Not mechanical, not multicoloured or dear
Six identical sides and no eraser atop my head.

I'd be one of the shorter pencils in the case,
Too much force with a sharpener and I would
snap,
I'd never push ahead of the pens, I'd know my
place
But count on me for a rhythm when you want to
tap tap tap!

My paint would be far from perfect; cracked and
chipped,
Sometimes my cheap wood might give you a
splinter,
I'd enjoy being rolled and whirled and flipped,
But I'd be deathly afraid of the fireplace in
winter.

For the writing exercise or maths problem, I
might be chosen last,
But I know I'm the lucky pencil you reach for in
that exam you need to pass.

Be Still

The alcohol evaporates tickling my nasal
passages as it goes,
I watch the vein thicken, and feel the valve
within it close
The tourniquet is pulled firm and tight,
The blood that fills my tube is warm and bright,
He doesn't flinch when I pierce his skin,
This prick is nothing, compared to the pain he is
in
Skin yellow, eyes sunken and belly bloated,
Poisoned by a sticky, black suffocating ooze; his
liver, lungs, brain coated
His breathing is laboured, his voice so weak,
There is a deep indentation where there was
once a cheek.

No blood test or scan is needed to know he is not
well,
And no loved ones have come to visit as far as I
can tell
He does not scream, he is quiet in illness,
There is not long now, he is close to stillness.

The Same

What is truly the difference between you and
me?
Aside from a piece of paper that states I have a
degree.
Or the two initials that trail behind my name -
M.D.

I am not built in any different way,
The suffering, illness, pain and death I see each
day,
Is just as difficult as you might think,

Me and my friends are pushed to the brink.

Polynya

A polynya is a special and little known thing,
An oasis found in the most unlikely of places,
A hotspot of life in a frozen dessert
Supporting, steadfast and staunch.

A polynya is you.

Core Memory

With surgical precision she slices the apple,
Unnaturally glossy pink skin with yellow
freckles,
Firm flesh oozing a sugary syrup

The first bite is as sweet and crisp as she
imagined
The sound of chewing is comforting

She holds the knife up to her face
And runs the smooth edge of the blade against
her tongue
The coolness makes her shiver
Tasty

Sunday Morning

Viscous batter hits the pan with a sizzle
Almost perfectly circular, slowly rising
Tiny bubbles erupt from within
Craters pockmark the surface

A quick flip reveals a smooth underside
Golden-brown and lubricated by burnt butter
The distinctive smell of this familiar Sunday
breakfast fills the air

Blueberries
Strawberries
Maple Syrup

And a stack of pancakes

Yellow and Blue

The man in the long yellow coat walks next to
me
Though he never speaks, sometimes I hear a
voice
It's the one that tells the truth

The wind tickles the pink cherry blossoms
The lucky ones take flight, they are free
The man watches them, envy gleaming in his
eyes

His navy cargo pants are decorated with pockets
Zips, buttons and velcro hide small treasures
The voices have led him on this discovery

I carry his favourite tools in a red satchel
They guide him to where he needs to go
The legend to read the invisible map

He is the architect of my journey
And the giver of happiness
The gifts he recovers are carefully placed
Waiting to be found by the man in the long blue
coat

Thirsty

A glass of water sits on the coffee table
It is untouched
But when he roars and sneers
It shrinks
When his fist slams onto the table
It wobbles
And when he throws the empty bottle of beer
across the room
It breaks

At Sea

My arms paddle weakly in a unknown sea,
Not quite sure what lies beneath the surface
I'm pulled by two equally powerful, yet
opposing currents,
Which way to the safety of land?

She deploys a buoy and set of flags,
Be careful
They might be traps

Her

Her hips are bony
Her chest is flat
Her knees are knobbly
Her clothes are loose

Why are you complaining, you're so thin

App

Swipe left. Swipe left. Swipe left.
Too much choice, not enough options.
Everybody's here.
There's no one here.

Orange Shorts

I pull at the loose orange thread that hangs from
the hem
A new pair of shorts, a gift unwanted
Reluctantly accepted with an untruthful smile
The thread falls away, stiches come undone

Her eagle eye has caught me
She raises her right hand and slaps my wrist
Chunky gold rings against bony protrusions
It stings

Stupid, ungrateful girl she spits
High heels pierce the carpet as she walks away

Ba

A plate piled high with shortbread biscuits
Sweet tea in 4 cups
With dainty handles and chipped paint
Doilies arranged in no particular pattern
Underneath a sticky, clear plastic table cloth

Have another biscuit
Have another cup of tea
I can make you something else
Stay a while longer

Thanks, Ba

Kind regards

Long, acryllic nails against a keyboard
Sticky notes on the monitor
A4 spiral notebook

Chair height adjusted
Coffee break
Ergonomic stretches

A passive-aggressive reply all
Back up cc'ed in
Forwarded to a supporter

Kind regards

Edit

Six people read the sentence I wrote.
They each change a word.
The meaning hasn't changed.
But it is unrecognisable.

Date night

Wet hair drips on the old carpet
The hairdryer has stopped working
The hot water has run out
She's running late

He's waiting